3-D Bible Stories

With 3-D Illustrations by
**Otherworld Artyfax, Digi-Rule, Inc.
and John Olsen**

Written by
Mary Ruberry

3-D Revelations Publishing
Newport Beach, CA, USA

ISBN: 0-9641811-4-2
Library of Congress Catalog Card Number: 94-060905

Design and Layout by Mary Francis-DeMarois
The Creative Spark, San Clemente, CA

First Printing, September 1994
Printed in the United States of America

Also from 3-D Revelations:
"THE 3-D NIGHT BEFORE CHRISTMAS"
by Clement C. Moore*——3-D Illustrations by John Olsen

"FATHER FORGIVE THEM" 3-D PRINT
A 22x28 inch 3-D print of the front cover crucifixion scene, titled
"Father Forgive Them", by Bohdan, is available through your local
Christian retailer. For a retailer near you write:
3-D Revelations
537 Newport Center Drive, Suite 282
Newport Beach, CA 92660 USA

NEW AMERICAN STANDARD Bible used in reference

Grateful thanks to Norma Collins

Artists credits:
Ryan Jones, Marie DeLeon, OtherWorld Artyfax
Bohdan, Digi-Rule, Inc.
John Olsen, Infix Technologies

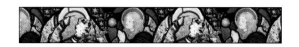 # INTRODUCTION

We have selected a variety of beloved stories from the Bible to illustrate with the captivating phenomenon of 3-D artwork. The visual nature of the miracles contained within each story lend themselves well to these 3-D wonderworkings.

3-D stereogram art is a fascinating production of the computer age whereby software fractures a 3-D model which our eyes, upon '3-D viewing', put back together thereby creating the holographic perception of depth (see instruction page "How to See in 3-D").

We recognize the sacred and complete nature of the Holy Bible and hope with this selection of stories and illustrations to bring a new way of viewing these Biblical wonders.

Special thanks to Reverend Bill Woolsey

How to See in 3-D

Viewing these 3-D stereograms requires that you adjust your vision in a most unusual way. You'll see the submerged 3-D images when your focal point is about 10 feet beyond the illustration. "Looking through" the illustration is how many viewers describe the sensation.

Your patience and relaxation are key elements to finding your 3-D vision. It usually takes five or more attempts using these instructions to see in 3-D, so stay with it!

1) Hold any illustration about 2 inches from your nose for one minute. Your vision will be blurry but allow your eyes to relax and "look through" the page. You may notice that even though your vision is blurred, you will have a sense that there is depth in the illustration.

2) Very slowly, without refocusing or blinking, pull the illustration away from your face. As your eyes start to lock-on to the 3-D image you will be amazed at how comfortable and clear the image becomes. Don't be alarmed if it doesn't happen for you right away. Simply start over and allow your eyes to relax even more. With a little practice it will become easy to find your 3-D vision. You'll enjoy using your new 3-D vision to explore the details in the following illustrations.

 # CONTENTS

THE OLD TESTAMENT

THE NEW TESTAMENT

The Lord bless you, and keep you,
The Lord make His face shine on you;
And be gracious to you;
The Lord lift up His countenance on you,

And give you peace.   *Numbers 6:24-26*

THE OLD TESTAMENT

 CREATION

In the beginning God created everything. The formless earth was empty and covered by an endless black ocean. God's breath moved over the waters and they stirred. He said, "Let there be light." And light appeared.

God made land and continents and covered the land with vegetation. He also made the heavenly lights so that night and day could be distinguished. God made creatures to populate the planet and told them to be fruitful and multiply.

Then God created people in His own image and blessed them. He told them to fill the earth. And God saw all that He had made and, behold, it was good.

God's creation took six days, and on the seventh day He rested.

Across the earth
life's abundance grew and spread,
and the manifest glory of God
knew no bounds.

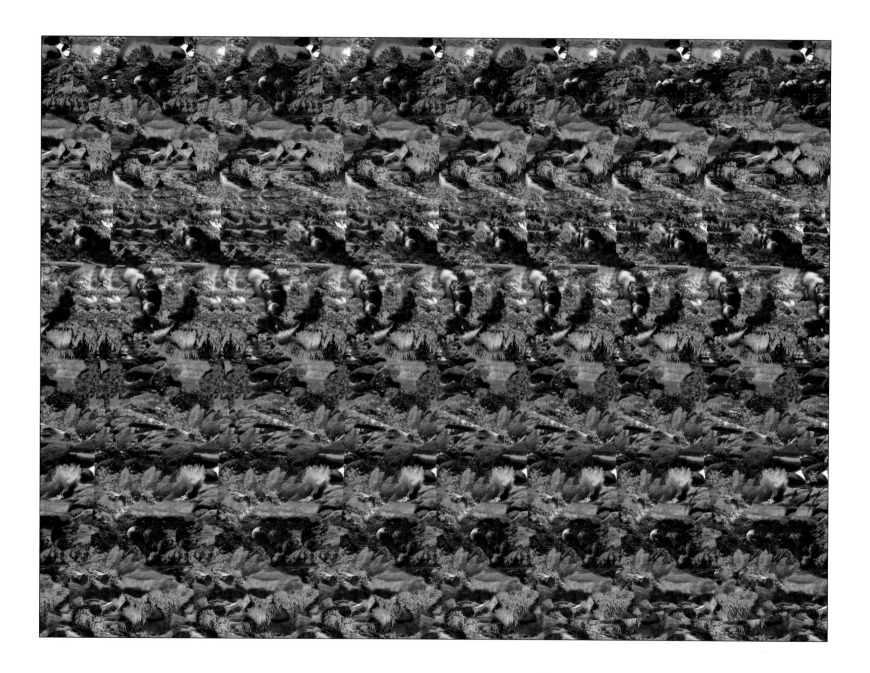

11

 Noah and the Ark

When people lived all over the world, their thoughts became wicked and violence spread everywhere. God came to regret having made humanity, and decided that He would destroy the people of the earth because of their evil ways. But God was pleased with Noah.

Noah had three sons and was the only good man of his time. The rest of humanity was evil in God's sight.

God told Noah that he was going to destroy the world but that He would make a covenant with him. He instructed Noah to build a large boat. Then God told Noah to take his wife and family, along with one pair of every creature on earth, and enter into the boat. This great ark was to be their refuge from the floods which God was going to send upon the earth.

Noah did everything as God commanded. The rains came and continued until all the earth was covered in deep water. Even the highest mountaintops were covered in water, and everything on earth died.

But God did not forget Noah and his family. He stopped the rains and sent a wind to dry the land. Noah sent a dove out of the boat to seek dry land, but since the land was still covered in water, the dove had no place to light and returned to the ark. Noah waited seven days and sent the dove out again. This time it came back with an olive branch in its beak. After waiting another seven days, Noah sent the dove out, and this time it did not return.

God said to Noah, "Go out from the boat, with your wife and family and take along all the birds and animals so they may reproduce and spread over all the earth." The contents of the ark were emptied so the earth might be filled with living creatures.

Noah and his family were very happy that the flood was over and gave thanks to the Lord.

And God promised that He would never again send such a devastating flood upon the earth.

"While the earth remains,
seedtime and harvest,
and cold and heat,
and summer and winter,
and day and night,
shall not cease."

Genesis 8:22

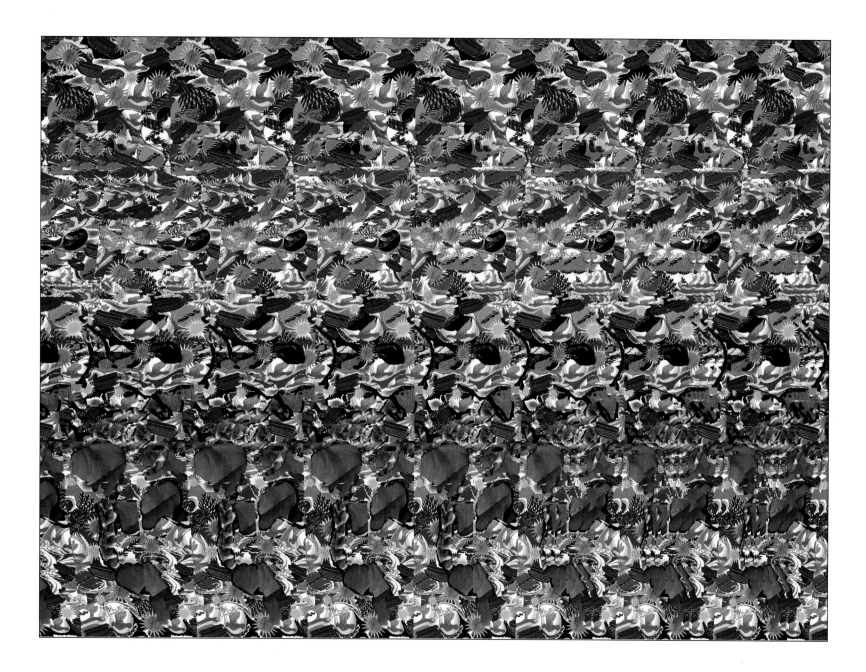

MOSES

The Israelites came to live in Egypt as slaves, but always longed to escape from their cruel bondage into the land that God promised them. One of the Israelites, Moses, found favor in the eyes of God and was greatly blessed.

One day as Moses was tending his flock, God spoke to him from a bush. The bush was engulfed in flames but did not appear to be burning up. Moses was afraid, but God comforted him and gave him a very important message. God directed Moses to lead the Israelites out of Egypt and into the promised land.

Moses doubted that anyone would believe what he said. But God gave him miracles to show to the Israelites and to Pharaoh so they would believe him. However, God warned Moses that the heart of Pharaoh would be hardened to the plea of the Israelites.

 PASSOVER

As God instructed, Moses went to the Israelites and delivered God's message. He showed them the miracles with which God had entrusted him, and the people were in awe. They knew that Moses represented the true God.

But the heart of Pharaoh was hardened and he refused to let the Israelites go. God sent many plagues upon the Egyptians, and they suffered greatly. But still Pharaoh would not agree to let the Israelites go.

Finally God gave instructions that the Israelites were to sacrifice a goat or sheep and put the blood on the doorposts and above the doors. They were told to eat the animals with unleavened bread and bitter herbs. God told the people to continue the festival of Passover and to pass the tradition on to their children.

God sent His Angel of Death throughout Egypt, killing the firstborn of each family in the land. But the angel passed over the homes that were marked with blood, and thus the Israelites were spared.

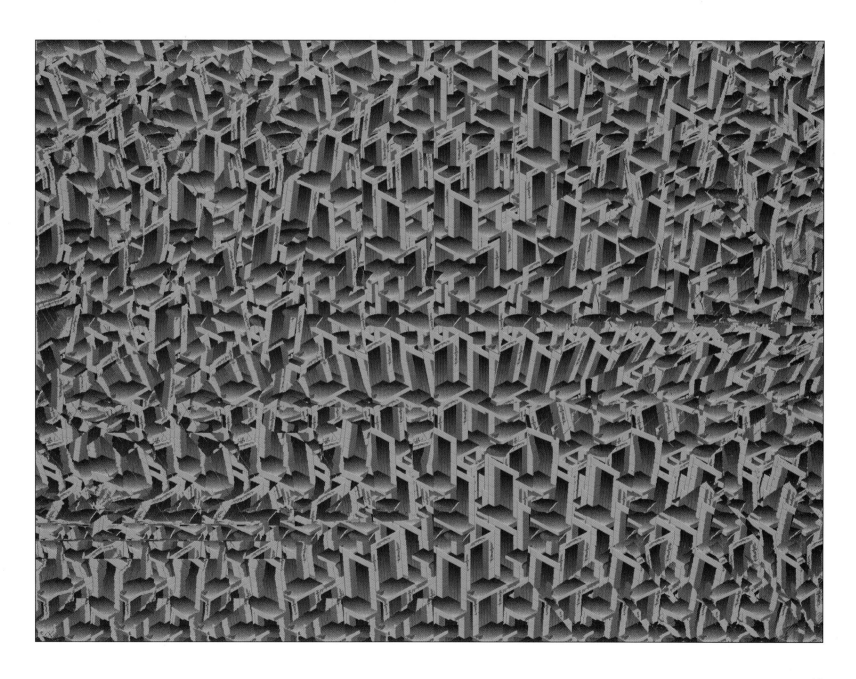

 # EXODUS

The Egyptians could not withstand the will of God any longer. Their stubborness in refusing to release the Israelites brought ruin to their land. Finally they agreed to let the Israelites flee from Egypt. So the Israelites left Egypt with all their belongings. They went out into the desert, following the path that God directed them to take.

After the Israelites fled from Egypt, Pharaoh changed his mind because he did not want to lose the Israelite slaves. He sent his army in pursuit, and they came upon the Israelites near the Red Sea. When the Israelites saw the great army of Pharaoh, they feared for their lives. But Moses held his hand over the sea and the water parted. The Israelites crossed the sea on dry ground between two walls of water, but the Egyptians were in close pursuit.

God caused the wheels of the Egyptian chariots to stick in the mud, and then He told Moses to close the water of the sea over them. The Egyptian army was swallowed by the waters of the Red Sea, and the Israelites were saved.

"Sing to the Lord
for He is highly exalted;
the horse and rider
He has hurled into the sea."

Exodus 15:1

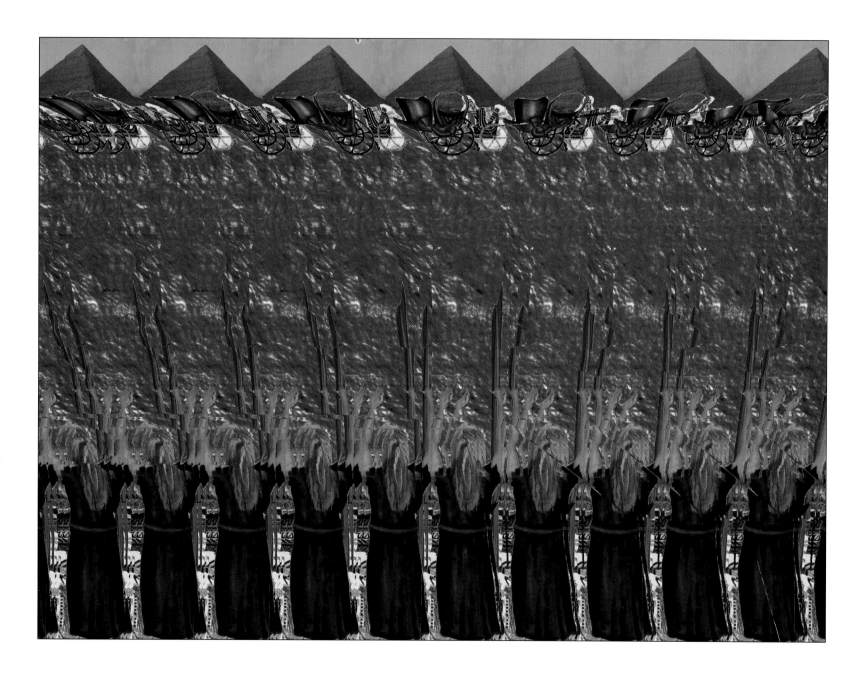

 GOD'S COVENANT

The Israelites traveled through the desert and experienced much hardship. But God stayed with His people and gave them water to drink and manna from heaven to keep them from starving.

Eventually the Israelites set up camp at the base of Mount Sinai, and Moses went up on the mountain to speak with God. God told Moses that He wanted to hand down His laws for the people to follow. God directed Moses to prepare the people to receive the word of God.

On the appointed day all the Israelites gathered at the foot of Mount Sinai, and a thick cloud appeared on the mountain. The people trembled, as loud trumpet blasts pierced the air and the mountain was covered in smoke. From the cloud of smoke, God spoke to the multitude.

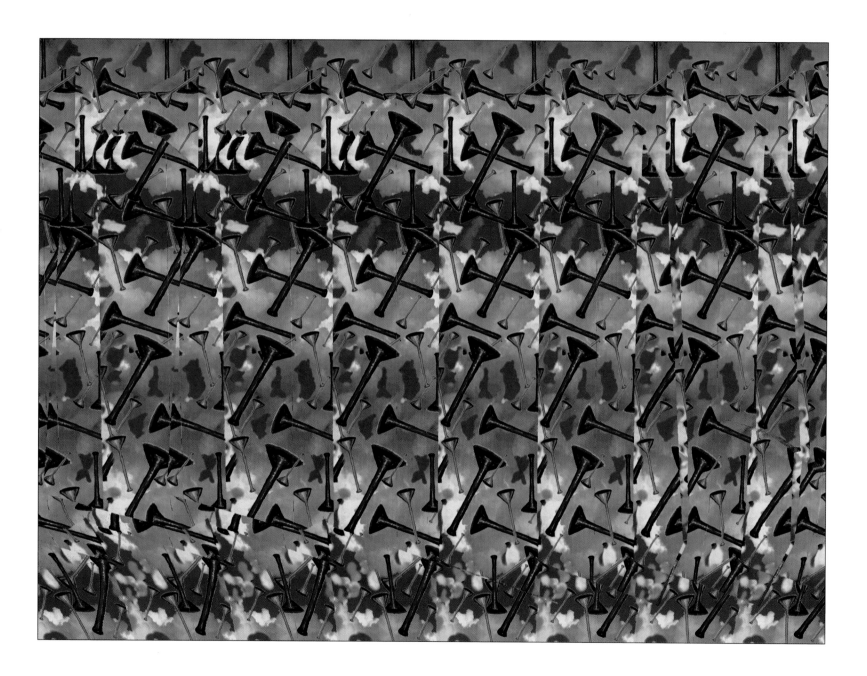

 ARK OF THE COVENANT

These are the Ten Commandments that God gave to the Israelites:

1. I am the true God.

2. Worship no God but Me.

3. Do not misuse My name.

4. Observe the Sabbath.

5. Respect your mother and father.

6. Do not commit murder.

7. Do not commit adultery.

8. Do not steal.

9. Do not falsely accuse another.

10. Do not desire another's possessions.

Moses went up on the mountain, and God gave him two stone tablets containing the laws God wrote for the instruction of the people. Moses stayed on the mountain for forty days and nights, and the people began to think he would never return. They decided to make a calf of gold, as a new god to lead them out of the desert. Then they reveled in adoration to their idol.

When Moses came down from the mountain, he was very angry because of what the people had done. He broke the stone tablets on the ground and then destroyed the golden calf. But God forgave the people and gave Moses new commandment tablets, which were placed in a beautiful wooden ark. The Israelites carried the ark and tablets with them wherever they went, as a reminder of God's covenant with His chosen people.

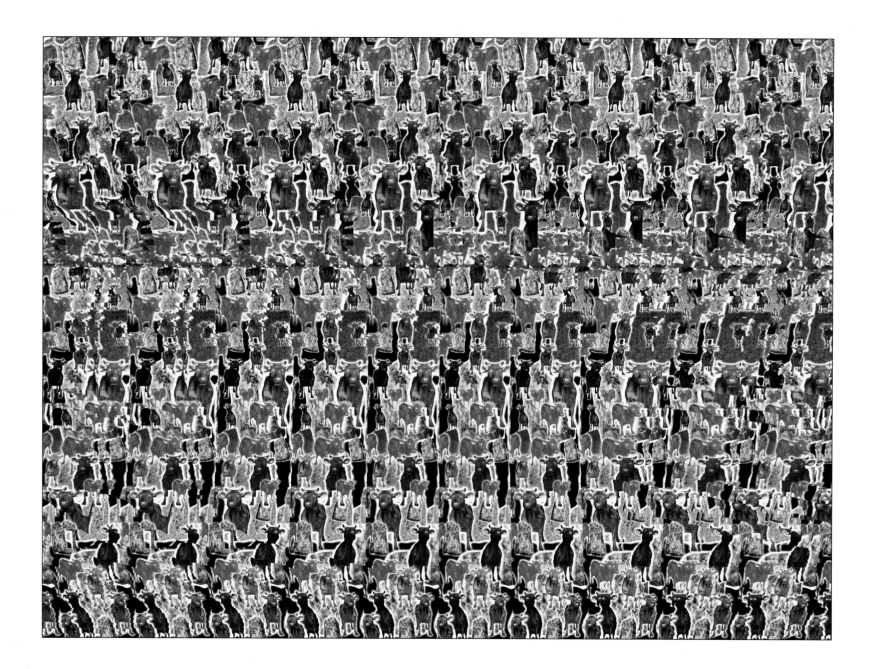

THE DEATH OF MOSES
AND THE ISREALITES' ENTRY INTO THE PROMISED LAND

After many years of hardship, the Israelites finally reached the end of their journey. But before they crossed the River Jordan, Moses died while gazing into the land that God had promised to them and their ancestors—a lush green land where "milk and honey flowed." So the people came out of the desert to enter their new homeland . . . but without Moses, their great leader.

The Song of Moses
Earth and sky, hear my words,
listen closely to what I say.
My teaching will fall like drops of rain
and form on the earth like dew.
My words will fall like showers on young plants,
like gentle rain on tender grass.
I will praise the name of the Lord,
and His people will tell of His greatness.

Deuteronomy 32:1-3

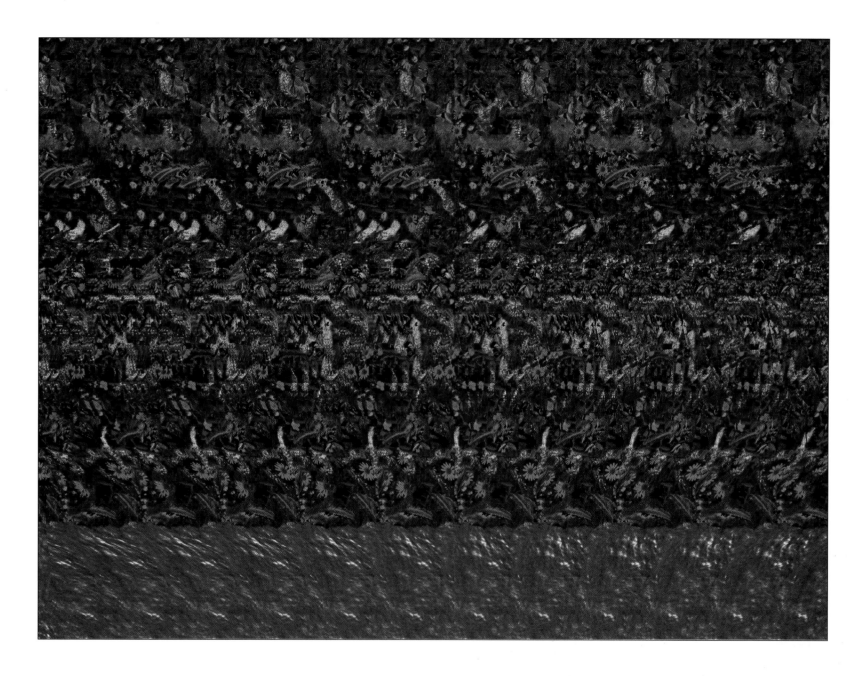

 JONAH

God came to Jonah and told him to travel to the city of Nineveh and urge the people there to turn from their evil ways. But, instead, Jonah ran from the word of God and boarded a ship. When the ship got out to sea, a terrible storm arose. The ship would have sunk, but Jonah, knowing he was the reason for the storm, told the men to throw him overboard, which they finally did.

The waters immediately grew calm, and a huge fish that God sent swam up and swallowed Jonah. Jonah stayed in the belly of the fish for three days and nights, praying to God to deliver him. God granted his deliverance and the fish released Jonah on dry land.

Jonah rejoiced at his freedom and went straight to the city of Nineveh, where he delivered God's message of repentance.

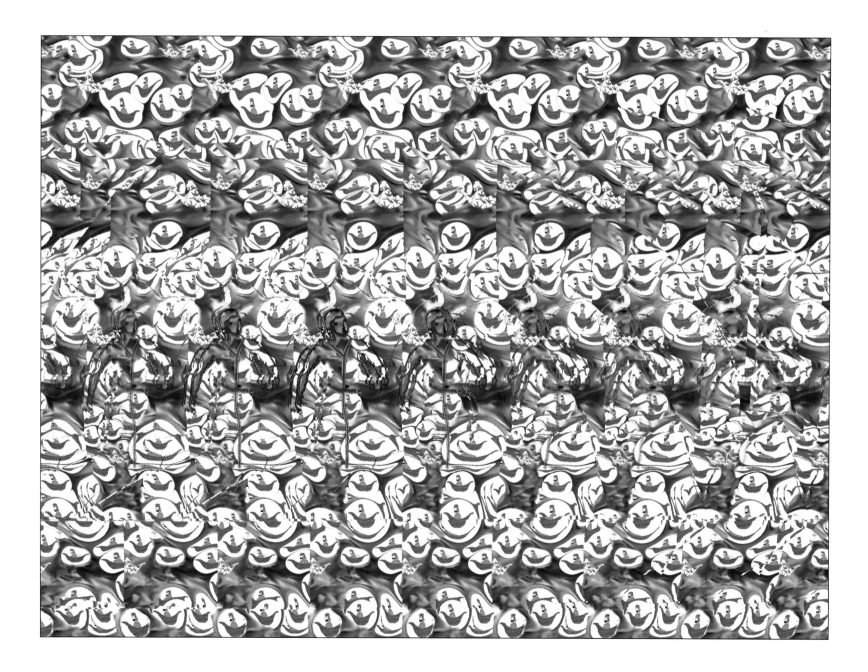

 THE 23RD PSALM

The Lord is my shepherd; I shall not want.

He maketh me to lie down in green pastures: He leadeth me beside the still waters.

He restoreth my soul: He leadeth me in the paths of righteousness for His name's sake.

Yea, though I walk through the valley of the shadow of death, I will fear no evil:

for Thou art with me; Thy rod and Thy staff they comfort me.

Thou preparest a table before me in the presence of mine enemies:

Thou anointest my head with oil;

my cup runneth over.

Surely goodness and mercy shall follow me all the days of my life:

and I will dwell in the house of the Lord forever.

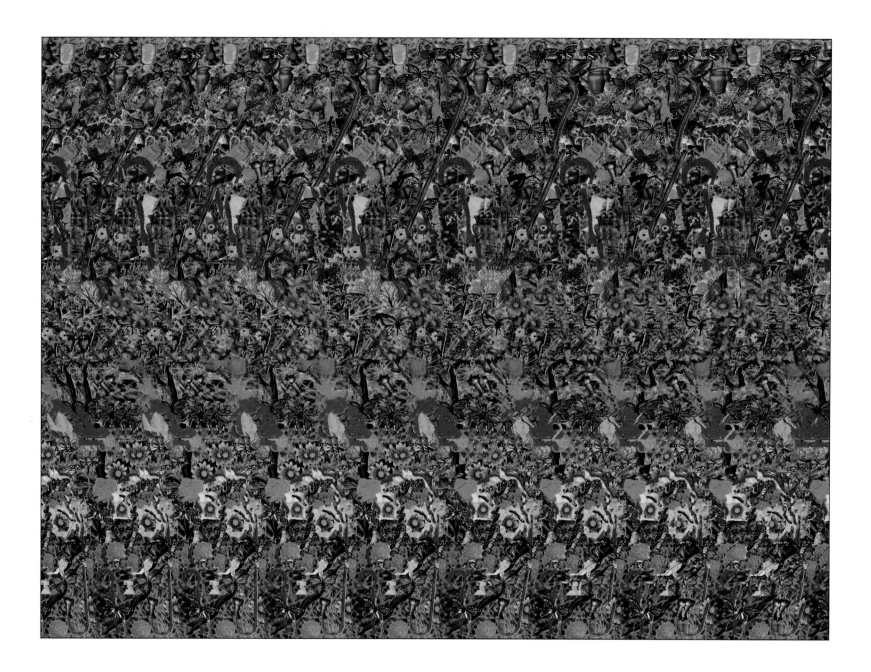

ECCLESIASTES

To everything there is a season, and a time to every purpose under heaven:

A time to be born, and a time to die;

a time to plant, and a time to pluck up that which is planted;

A time to kill, and a time to heal;

a time to break down, and a time to build up;

A time to weep, and a time to laugh;

a time to mourn, and a time to dance;

A time to cast away stones, and a time to gather stones together;

a time to embrace, and a time to refrain from embracing;

A time to get, and a time to lose;

a time to keep, and a time to cast away;

A time to rend, and a time to sew;

a time to keep silence, and a time to speak;

A time to love, and a time to hate;

a time of war, and a time of peace.

EZEKIEL
AND THE VALLEY OF THE DRY BONES

God spoke to the people through a great prophet named Ezekiel. Ezekiel delivered God's messages to the people so they could learn to walk in God's way.

God showed many visions to Ezekiel so he could gain greater wisdom. During one vision God placed Ezekiel in a valley filled with dry bones. God told Ezekiel to prophesy to the dry bones so they could hear the words of the Lord and come to life. As Ezekiel prophesied to the bones, he heard a rattling sound, and the bones came together to form skeletons. Ezekiel watched as muscle formed over the bones and they were covered with skin. But they had no breath. So God told Ezekiel to prophesy to the breath, causing it to fill the fallen ones so they could come alive. Ezekiel prophesied as God commanded, and breath came into the bodies. A large mass of people came to life and stood on their feet.

God spoke again to Ezekiel and said, "My people say, 'Our bones are dried up and our hope has perished.' But say to them, 'Thus says the Lord God, I will open your graves and bring you out. I will put My spirit into you, and you will be filled with the breath of life.'"

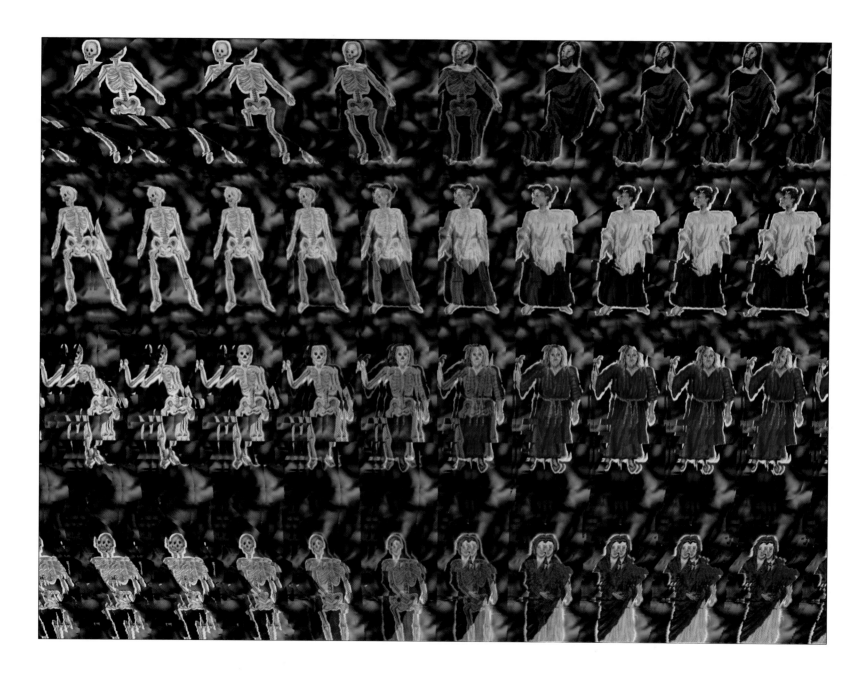

DANIEL
AND THE DEN OF LIONS

When the king of Babylon conquered Jerusalem, he selected Daniel to serve in his court. Daniel found favor with the king who elevated him to a high position. Many Babylonians were jealous of Daniel's success, so they plotted to bring about his ruin.

The Babylonians passed a law that if anyone worshiped any god but the king, they would be thrown into a pit of lions. Following his daily habit, Daniel was seen kneeling in prayer at an open window. The Babylonians denounced him to the king, and Daniel was thrown in the lions' den.

The king was distraught at Daniel's fate and couldn't sleep all night. Early the next morning the king went to the pit of lions and called out to Daniel, who answered that the lions would not hurt him because he was innocent.

"To Thee, O God of my fathers,
I give thanks and praise.
for Thou hast given me
wisdom and power."

Daniel 2:23

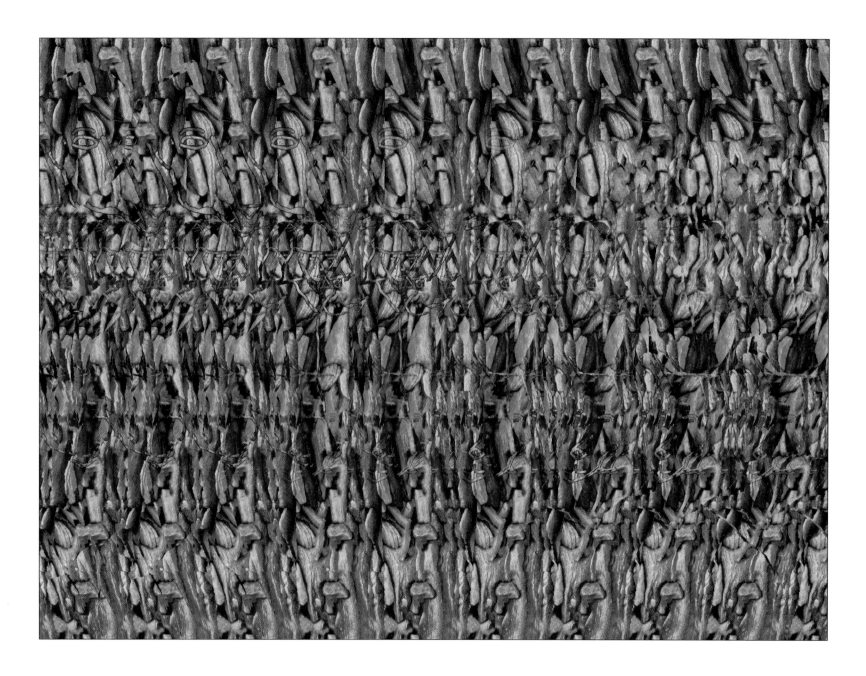

And it shall be said on that day,
"Lo, this is our God;
we have waited for Him, and He will save us.
This is the Lord;
we have waited for Him,
we will be glad and rejoice in His salvation."

Isaiah 25:9

THE NEW TESTAMENT

 # ANNUNCIATION OF MARY

God sent His angel Gabriel to a virgin named Mary, who was engaged to Joseph. The angel greeted Mary and told her she was favored by God. But she was troubled by his message, since she did not know what he meant. The angel comforted her and told her that she was to bear a son named Jesus, who would be called the Son of the Most High. The angel told her that God would give Him the throne of David, and His kingdom would have no end.

Mary wondered how she could bear a child, since she had never known a man. But Gabriel told her that the Holy spirit would come upon her, the power of the Most High would overshadow her and, therefore, her holy offspring would be called the Son of God. Gabriel said, "Nothing is impossible with God."

Mary responded that she was the Lord's servant and would do whatever God willed. So the angel departed.

And Mary raised her voice to heaven:
"My soul exalts in the Lord,
and my spirit rejoices in God my Savior."

Luke 1:46-47

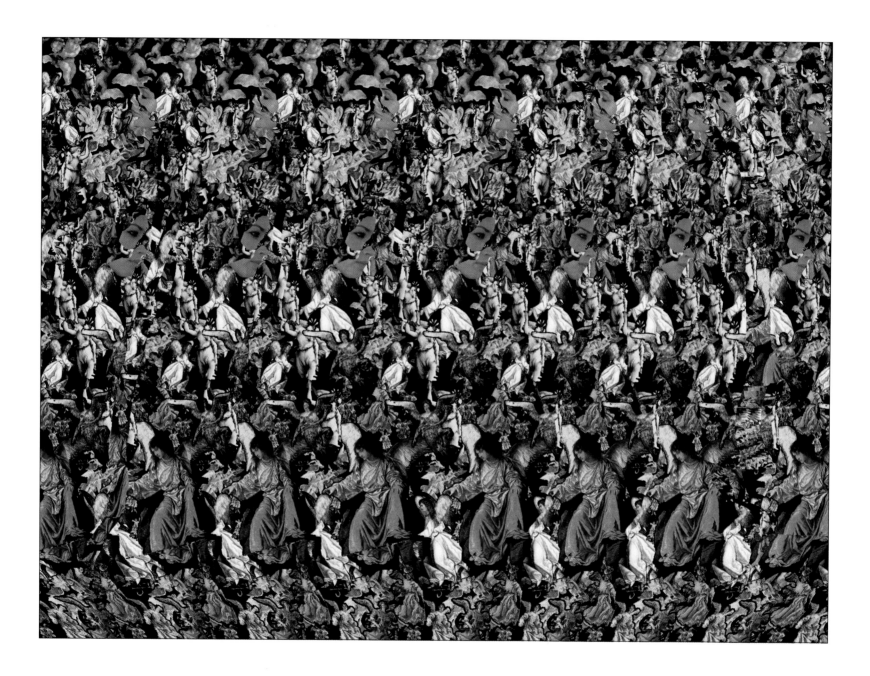

 THE BIRTH OF JESUS

When Joseph learned that his betrothed was with child, he planned to break the engagement. But an angel came to him in a dream and told him that the child was the Son of God, who would save the people from their sins. So Joseph married Mary, but kept her a virgin until after the boy was born.

✢

When Mary was heavy with child, she had to travel with Joseph from their home in Nazareth to the city of David, called Bethlehem. They were required to register there for the census, which was being taken of the entire Roman empire. All the inns were filled with travelers, so Joseph took Mary to rest in a stable. There in the stable she gave birth to Jesus, wrapped Him in cloth, and laid Him in a manger.

In the hills around Bethlehem, shepherds were tending their flocks. An angel of the Lord appeared to them, rejoicing with the happy news of Jesus' birth. Following the angel's guidance, the shepherds went into Bethlehem and found Mary, Joseph, and baby Jesus. They later returned to their flocks, praising God at the wonders they saw.

"Glory to God in the highest,
and on earth peace to men of goodwill."

Luke 2:14

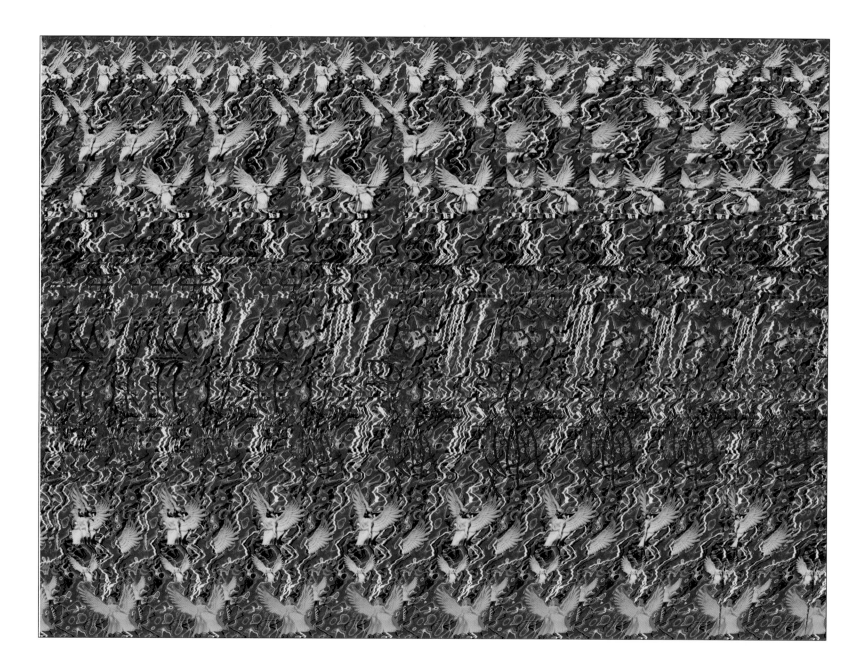

 # THE THREE WISE MEN

After Jesus was born, the Magi appeared from the East, following a very bright star. In Jerusalem, they asked where the King of the Jews had been born. They wanted to find Him and give Him homage. But when Herod the king heard about their inquiries, he was troubled and asked to see the three men. King Herod wrested information from them about this child king. He told them to report back to him on their return, so that he, too, might go to worship this new king.

So the wise men continued on their travels, still following the bright star, and finally found Jesus in Bethlehem. They fell on their knees, rejoicing at this great miracle, and presented Jesus with very valuable gifts of gold, frankincense, and myrrh.

But they were warned in a dream not to return to Herod, who meant the child harm. And they returned home by a different route.

THE MARRIAGE AT CANA

When Jesus was a young man, before He began His ministry, He went to a wedding in the town of Cana with His mother. At one point during the celebration, Mary learned that the host had run out of wine. Mary went to Jesus, saying, "They have no wine." But Jesus replied that His time had not yet come. Nevertheless, Mary told the servants to do whatever Jesus asked of them.

Because of His great love for His mother, Jesus could not refuse her request. He instructed the servants to fill large stone pots with water and then bring the pots to the head waiter. When the servants had done as Jesus told them, the waiter tasted the water which had been turned into wine. He marveled at its superior quality and remarked to the bridegroom, "Usually people serve their best wine first, but you have saved the good wine for last."

This first miracle, performed by Jesus at His mother's request, was a sign of His greatness to come and of the many miracles He would perform during His life on earth.

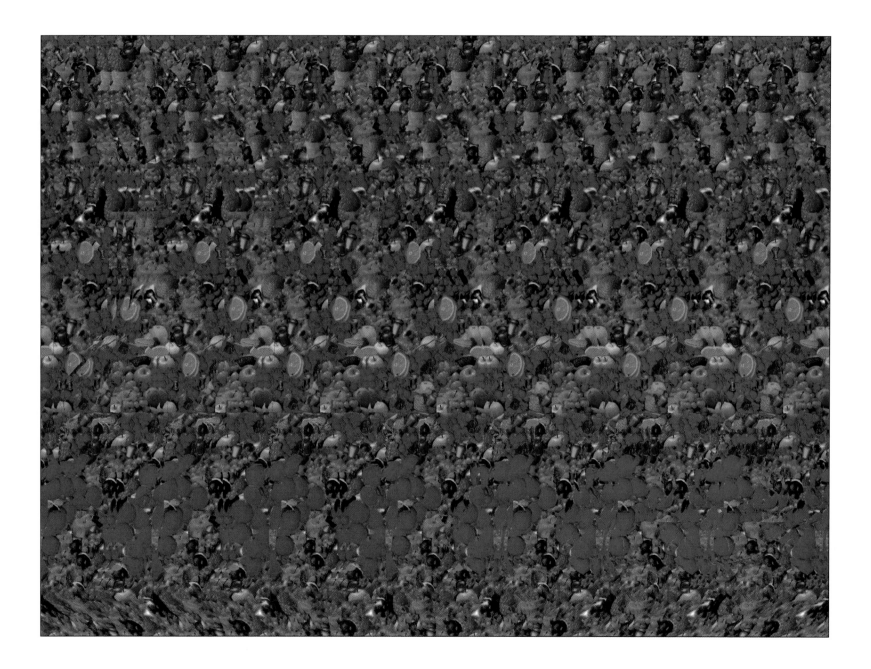

 THE LOAVES AND FISHES

As Jesus continued in His life of teaching and performing miracles, great throngs of people followed Him wherever He went. They were eager to hear His wisdom.

One evening Jesus' disciples urged Him to send the people away to buy food because it was late, and there was nothing available to eat. But Jesus did not want to send the people away, and said His disciples should feed the crowd. They told Him they only had five loaves of bread and two fish, which couldn't possibly feed so many people.

At least five thousand people had gathered to be with Jesus, and He told them to rest in the grass. He had the loaves and fish brought to Him, raised the bread and fish to heaven, blessed them, and broke the bread. He gave the food to His disciples and it was passed around. Everyone ate their fill, and the leftovers filled twelve baskets.

Then Jesus sent the multitude away and went to pray alone on a distant hill.

 JESUS WALKS ON WATER

While Jesus was still praying on the hilltop, His disciples boarded a small boat, as evening descended. Since it was getting dark and Jesus still had not come to them, they began to cross the Sea of Galilee to Capernaum.

But the sea became rough, and a strong wind blew. After a few hours they saw Jesus walking on the water toward their boat. At first they were frightened and thought He was a ghost. But Jesus calmed their fears, assuring them it was He. Peter responded to Jesus by saying, "Lord, if it is You, command me to come to You on the water." Jesus called Peter to come toward Him, and Peter also walked on the water.

But the wind rose again and Peter grew afraid. Then he began to sink and cry out to Jesus to save him. Jesus stretched out His hand and took hold of Peter, saying, "Oh, you of little faith. Why did you doubt?"

When they got in the boat, the wind stopped. And all the men worshiped Jesus, saying, "You are certainly God's Son!"

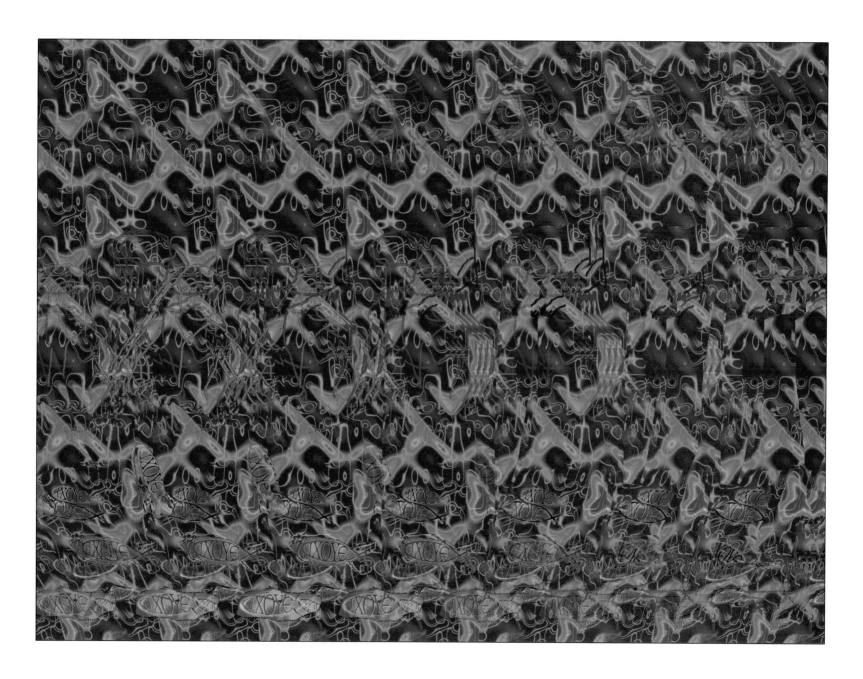

THE CRUCIFIXION

When Jesus' tasks were fulfilled, He knew the hour of His death was at hand. He celebrated the feast of passover sharing His last supper with the twelve disciples. Jesus washed their feet and lovingly gave them His final words of instruction and prayer.

One of His apostles, Judas, betrayed Him to the authorities for 30 pieces of silver. Eventually Jesus was condemned to die by hanging from a cross of wood.

On that darkest day, Jesus dragged a heavy cross up the Hill of Skulls, wearing a crown of thorns which the Roman soldiers mockingly placed on the head of this King of the Jews. The soldiers nailed Jesus' hands and feet to the cross and placed it upright between two thieves who were also being crucified.

It took many hours for Jesus to die in this painful way. His mother, her sister, Mary Magdalene, and John waited at His feet. When Jesus gave up His spirit, a Roman soldier pierced His side with a sword to make sure He was dead, and blood and water flowed from His side.

At the hour of Jesus' death, the earth shook and darkness obscured the sun. Observing this, the Roman soldier who was guarding Jesus said, "Surely this man was innocent."

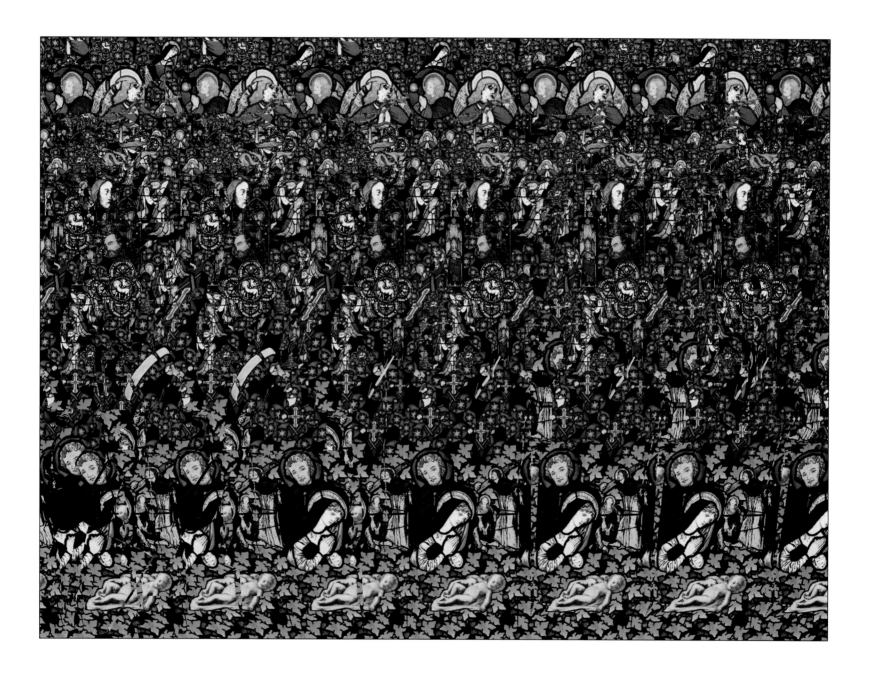

EASTER
JESUS RISES FROM THE DEAD

When the women came to anoint the body of Jesus three days after His death, they found that the stone had been rolled back and the tomb was empty. They became very upset, thinking that someone had stolen Jesus's body. To their bewilderment, an angel of the Lord appeared to them and asked why they sought the living among the dead. The angel told the women that Jesus was not there, but had risen, as the scriptures foretold.

Outside the tomb, Jesus appeared to them and asked them to tell His disciples that He would soon visit them in Galilee. The women delivered Jesus' message to the disciples and they were all filled with wonder, though still badly shaken by the persecution and death of their beloved Leader and Savior.

"To this end was I born,
and for this cause came I into the world,
that I should bear witness unto the truth.
Every one that is of the truth heareth my voice." *John 18:37*

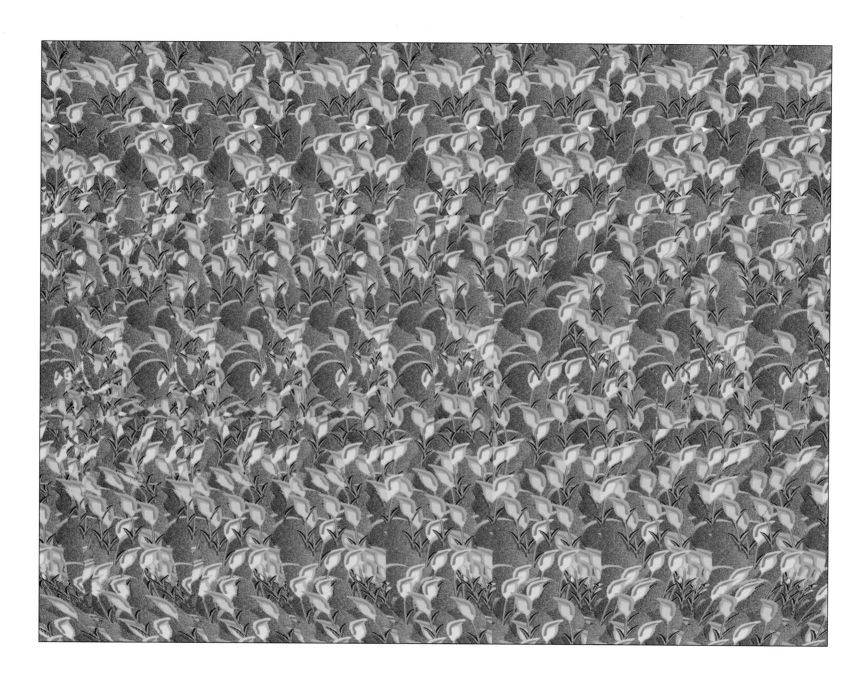

JESUS VISITS THE APOSTLES

Jesus came to the building where the apostles were hiding with all the doors and windows tightly shut. Jesus appeared to them and said, "Peace be with you." He showed them His hands and His side, and the apostles rejoiced at the miracle of His return.

But one apostle, Thomas, was not there when Jesus appeared. He did not believe the stories of the apostles. He said he would have to see the wounds of Jesus himself before he would believe Jesus was risen. So eight days later Jesus again appeared to the apostles in hiding, and showed his hands and side to Thomas, who was struck with awe at this wondrous occurrence.

Jesus said to Thomas, "You believe because you have seen. Blessed are those who did not see and yet believe."

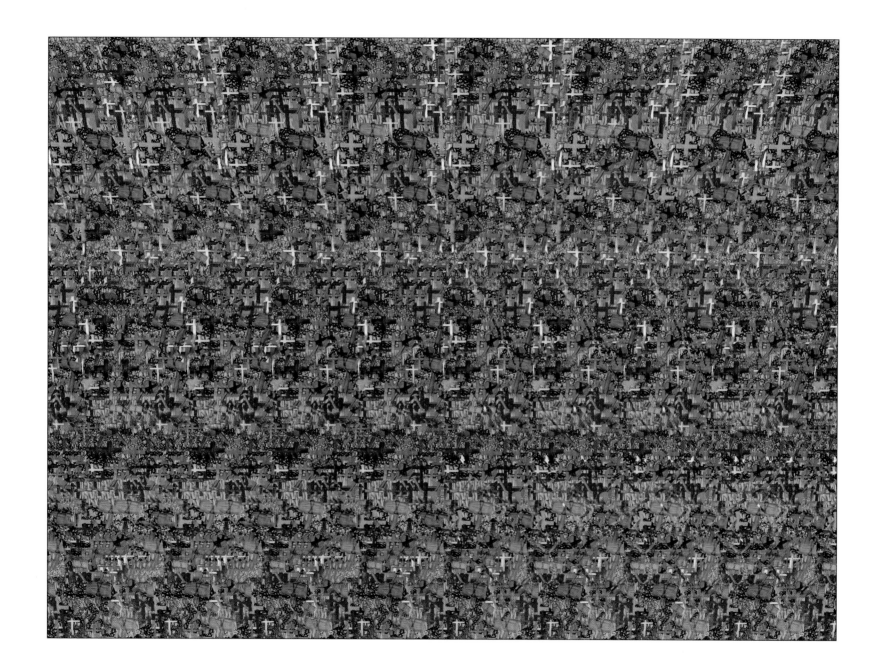

 THE ASCENSION OF JESUS

Jesus appeared to the apostles during a period of forty days. Finally He gathered them together and told them not to leave Jerusalem, but to wait for what the Father had promised. Jesus told them that John the Baptist had baptized with water, but that they would soon be baptized with the Holy Spirit. Jesus also told them they would gain great power when the Holy Spirit descended upon them, and that they would spread His word even to the remotest part of earth.

After Jesus spoke to the apostles with His last instructions, He was lifted up while the others looked on, and a cloud received Him out of their sight.

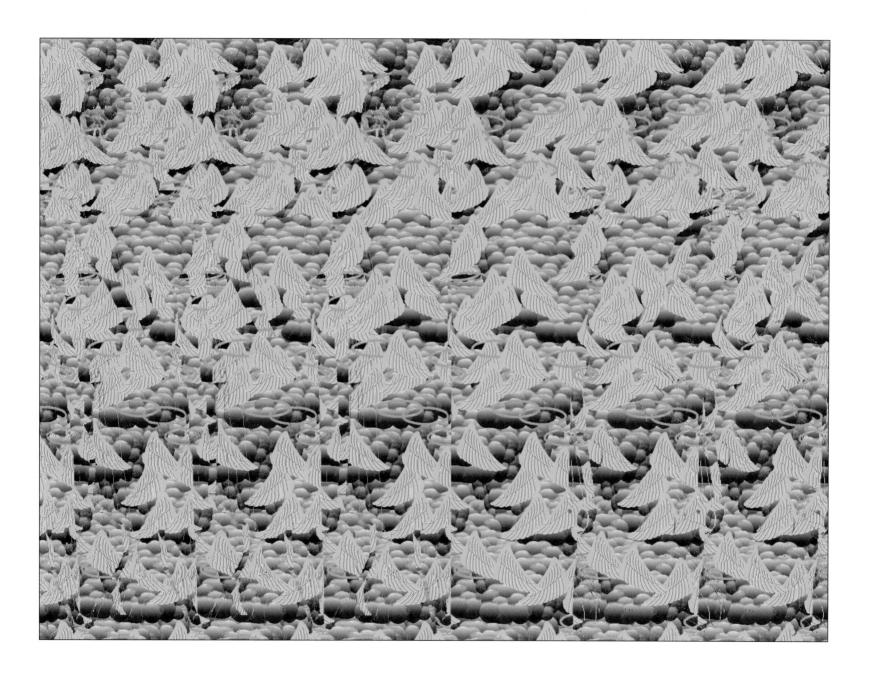

 # PENTECOST

When the day of Pentecost came, the apostles were gathered together. Suddenly the whole house was filled with the sound of a violent, rushing wind. Tongues of fire appeared and rested on each one, as they were filled with the Holy Spirit.

When the Holy Spirit filled them, they were blessed with the gift of speaking in many languages, and they went out into the streets, praising God.

At that time there were many Jews living in Jerusalem, who had come from all parts of the world. They heard the apostles speaking about God in their own tongues and marveled that God's word was being spread in so many languages.

So the word of God was spread by the apostles, as they traveled near and far. They carried out their tasks, as Jesus has instructed them, so that the peoples of the world would be filled with the salvation of new life.

61

GREY SCALE SOLUTIONS

page 11

page 13

page 15

page 17

page 19

page 21

page 23

page 25

page 27

page 29

page 31

page 33

page 35

page 37

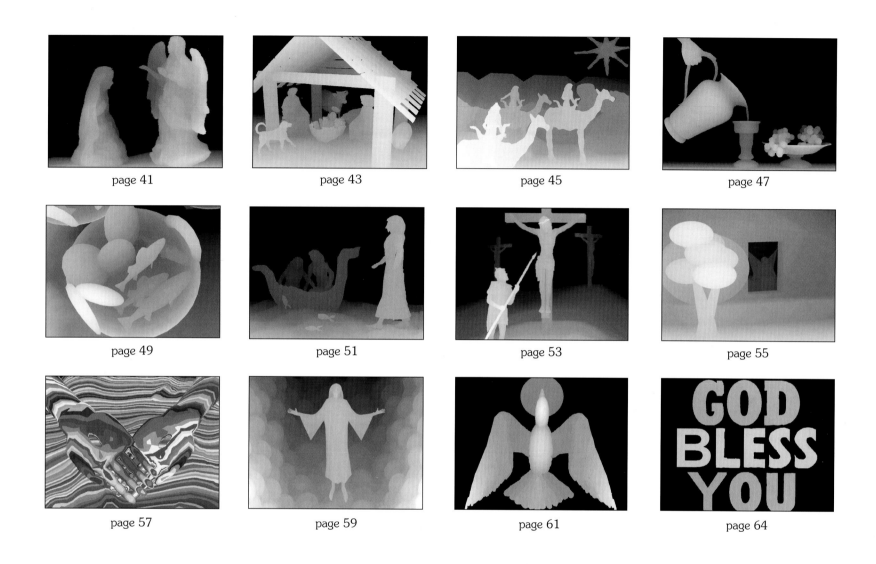

page 41

page 43

page 45

page 47

page 49

page 51

page 53

page 55

page 57

page 59

page 61

page 64

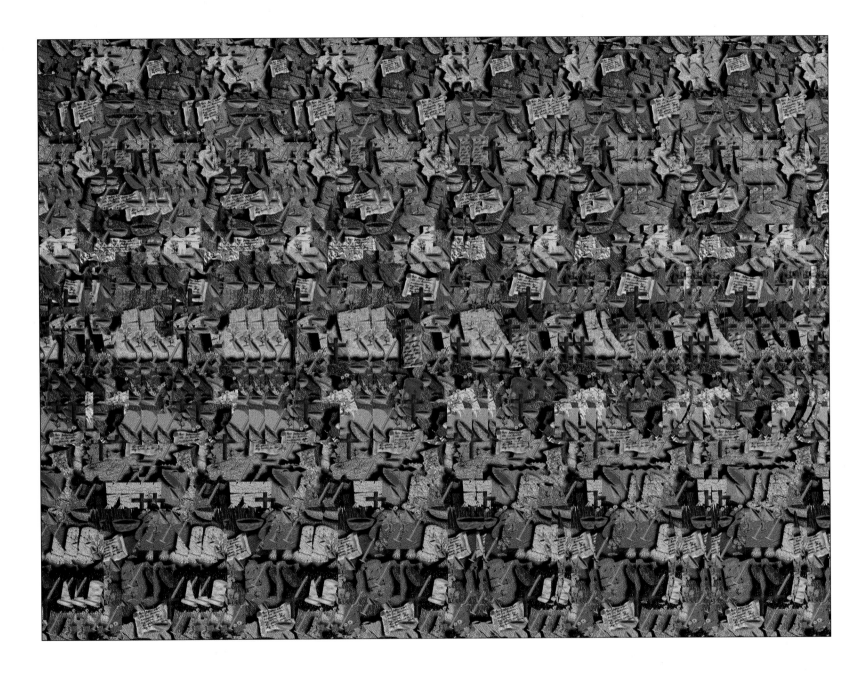